Classic Tales

Level 1

C000130503

Peach Boy

Retold by Sue Arengo
Illustrated by Tsugumi Yoshizawa

 Contents

OXFORD
UNIVERSITY PRESS

 It is summer in a village in Japan. An old man and woman eat dumplings. Yum! Nice little dumplings.

Then the old man goes to cut wood.
And the old woman goes to the river.

What a very big peach!

Suddenly the old woman
sees something. It's a peach.
A very big peach!

'What a very big peach!' she
says. 'Why is it in the river?'

The very big peach smells nice.
It smells of summer in Japan.

The woman catches it.

This peach smells wonderful.

'Mmm,' she says. 'This peach smells wonderful. I'm taking it home with me.'

'What a big peach!' says the old man. 'Let's eat it right now!'

But then they hear something. It's a baby!

'Stop!' says the baby. 'Don't cut me!'

There's a baby in the peach! A baby boy – a peach boy!

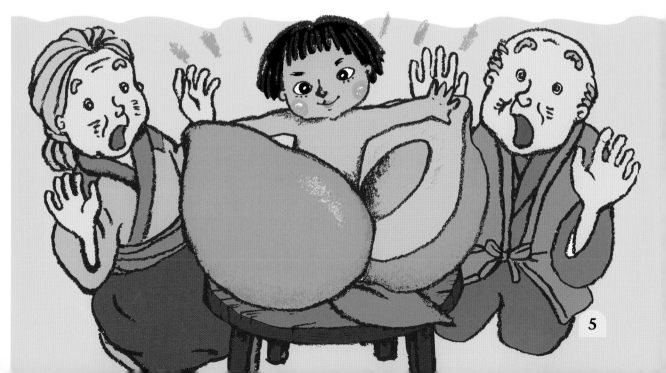

He is a wonderful baby, and he is happy. The old man and woman call him Momotaro – Peach Boy.

They give him nice little dumplings. So he grows big and strong.

The old man and woman are good
to Momotaro. So Momotaro is
good too.

Momotaro helps his mother and
father. He is a good boy. And he
is strong. He is very strong!

Then one day ogres come. Ogres come to the village.

Stamp! Stamp! Stamp!

They break things. They take things.

The ogres take the people's treasure. Then they stamp off into the sea.

Stamp! Stamp! Stamp!

Momotaro can see the ogres. They are going home. They are going home to Ogre Island.

'Mother, Father,' says Peach Boy. 'I want to fight the ogres. Give me some dumplings, please. And a big stick.'

So his mother gives him some dumplings. His father gives him a big stick.

'Goodbye,' they say. 'And good luck.'

Good luck.

Momotaro walks along. Then he sees a big dog.

Hi, *dog!*

'Hi, dog!' says Momotaro. 'I want to fight the ogres. Have a dumpling and come with me!'

So the dog eats the dumpling. Then it goes with him.

They walk along. Then they see
a pheasant.

'Hi, pheasant!' says Momotaro.
'We want to fight the ogres. Have
a dumpling and come with us!'

Have a dumpling!

So the pheasant eats the dumpling.
Then it goes with them.

They walk along. Then
they see a monkey.

Hi, *monkey!*

'Hi, monkey!' says Momotaro.
'We want to fight the ogres. Have
a dumpling and come with us!'

So the monkey eats the dumpling.
Then it goes with them.

'My friends,' says Momotaro, the
Peach Boy. 'Let's go to Ogre Island.
Let's fight the ogres.'

There's Ogre Island!

'There it is!' says Momotaro.
'There's Ogre Island! Look at the big
castle!'

Momotaro and his
friends look up.
They look up at
the big, big castle.

The castle door is
closed. But the
pheasant flies up.
It flies up into the
castle.

15

Help!

The pheasant fights
the ogres. The ogres
are afraid.

'Help!' they cry. 'Help!'

Then the monkey goes
up. It goes up into the
castle. It opens the door.

Momotaro and the dog run into the castle.

Bang! Bang! Bang! Momotaro fights the ogres with his stick.

The dog, the pheasant, and the monkey all fight. They all fight the ogres.

Bang! Bang! Bang!

The ogres are afraid.

'We are sorry,' they say. 'Please go.
Take your treasure and go.'

We are sorry.

Momotaro takes the treasure.

'Hurray!' he says. 'Good work,
my friends!'

Momotaro and his friends go home.
They go home with the treasure.

All the people shout, 'Hurray! Hurray!'

And the ogres never come back.

Exercises

1 Write the words.

1 It's an <u>island</u>.

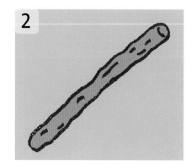

2 It's a _____.

3 It's a _____.

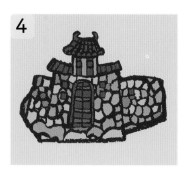

4 It's a _____.

5 It's an _____.

6 It's a _____.

2 Write the words.

> smells   takes   want   sees   ~~eat~~   goes

1 The old man and the old woman <u>eat</u> dumplings.
2 The old woman _____ to the river.
3 She _____ something in the river. It's a peach.
4 The peach _____ of summer in Japan.
5 The woman _____ the peach home with her.
6 The old man and the old woman _____ to eat the peach.

3 Answer the questions.

1 Is it an apple?

No, it isn't.

2 Is it a peach?

_____

3 Is it in the river?

_____

4 Is it small?

_____

5 Is there a monkey in it?

_____

6 Is there a baby in it?

_____

4 Number the sentences 1–7. Then write sentence 8.

☐ The monkey opens the castle door.

☐ Momotaro goes to Ogre Island with a dog, a pheasant, and a monkey.

1 The ogres come to Momotaro's village and take the people's treasure.

☐ The pheasant flies up into the castle.

☐ The ogres go home to Ogre Island.

☐ Momotaro and his friends fight the ogres.

☐ Momotaro's mother and father give him some dumplings and a big stick.

8 _____

Picture Dictionary

afraid *The ogre is afraid.*

dumplings

break

fight

castle

fly

catch

hear

cut

island

Japan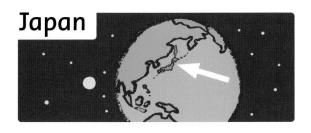

stick

ogre

strong *He is strong.*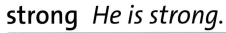

river

summer *It is summer.*

sea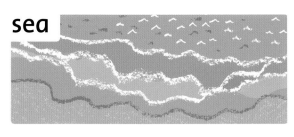

treasure

smell

village

stamp

23

Classic Tales

Classic stories retold for learners of English – bringing the magic of traditional storytelling to the language classroom

Level 1: 100 headwords

- The Enormous Turnip
- The Little Red Hen
- Lownu Mends the Sky
- The Magic Cooking Pot
- Mansour and the Donkey
- Peach Boy
- The Princess and the Pea
- Rumpelstiltskin
- The Shoemaker and the Elves
- Three Billy-Goats

Level 2: 150 headwords

- Amrita and the Trees
- Big Baby Finn
- The Fisherman and his Wife
- The Gingerbread Man
- Jack and the Beanstalk
- Thumbelina
- The Town Mouse and the Country Mouse
- The Ugly Duckling

Level 3: 200 headwords

- Aladdin
- Goldilocks and the Three Bears
- The Little Mermaid
- Little Red Riding Hood

Level 4: 300 headwords

- Cinderella
- The Goose Girl
- Sleeping Beauty
- The Twelve Dancing Princesses

Level 5: 400 headwords

- Beauty and the Beast
- The Magic Brocade
- Pinocchio
- Snow White and the Seven Dwarfs

All *Classic Tales* have an accompanying
- **e-Book with Audio Pack** containing the book and the e-book with audio, for use on a computer or CD player. Teachers can also project the e-book onto an interactive whiteboard to use it like a Big Book.
- **Activity Book and Play** providing extra language practice and the story adapted as a play for performance in class or on stage.

For more details, visit
www.oup.com/elt/readers/classictales

OXFORD
UNIVERSITY PRESS

Great Clarendon Street, Oxford, OX2 6DP, United Kingdom

Oxford University Press is a department of the University of Oxford. It furthers the University's objective of excellence in research, scholarship, and education by publishing worldwide. Oxford is a registered trade mark of Oxford University Press in the UK and in certain other countries

© Oxford University Press 2011

The moral rights of the author have been asserted

2015 2014 2013 2012
10 9 8 7 6 5 4 3 2

ISBN: 978 0 19 423858 8

This *Classic Tale* title is available as an e-Book with Audio Pack
ISBN: 978 0 19 423861 8

Also available: *Peach Boy* Activity Book and Play
ISBN: 978 0 19 423859 5

Printed in China

This book is printed on paper from certified and well-managed sources.

ACKNOWLEDGEMENTS
Illustrated by: Tsugumi Yoshizawa/ARTas1.com